Your Body and You

TAKING CARE OF YOUR BODY

By Anita Ganeri

Illustrated by Vera Popova

PowerKiDS press

Published in 2025 by The Rosen Publishing Group, Inc.
2544 Clinton Street, Buffalo, NY 14224

Credits

Series editor: Julia Bird
Illustrator: Vera Popova
Packaged by: Collaborate

Note to parents and teachers: every effort has been made by the Publishers to ensure websites are suitable for children, that they are of the highest educational value, and that they contain no inappropriate or offensive material. However, because of the nature of the Internet, it is impossible to guarantee that the contents of these sites will not be altered. We strongly advise that Internet access is supervised by a responsible adult.

Cataloging-in-Publication Data

Names: Ganeri, Anita, 1961-, author. | Popova, Vera, illustrator.
Title: Taking care of your body / by Anita Ganeri, illustrated by Vera Popova.
Description: Buffalo, NY : Powerkids Press, 2025. | Series: Your body and you |
Includes glossary and index.
Identifiers: ISBN 9781499445527 (pbk.) | ISBN 9781499445534 (library bound) |
ISBN 9781499445541 (ebook)
Subjects: LCSH: Hygiene--Juvenile literature. | Health--Juvenile literature.
Classification: LCC RA780.G326 2025 | DDC 613--dc23

Manufactured in the United States of America

CPSIA Compliance Information: Batch #CSPK25. For further information contact Rosen Publishing at 1-800-237-9932.

CONTENTS

BODY CARE

Think of everything you do during a day. From the time you get up, you're busy.

You go to school.

You play sports.

You do homework.

On the weekend, you're probably just as busy.

You might go for a bike ride.

You might dance in a show.

Your body works hard, day and night, so you can do all these things. It is important to keep your body well and strong by looking after yourself. This means eating healthy food, drinking plenty of water, keeping fit, and getting enough rest.

GOOD FOOD

Your busy body uses up lots of energy. Energy comes from the food you eat.

As you grow up, your body changes. This uses up more energy, and you probably feel hungry a lot of the time! This tells you your body needs refueling, so what are the best things to eat?

On this plate you can get an idea of how much of each kind of food you should eat.

To keep active and healthy, a balanced diet is best. This means eating a mixture of different kinds of foods. Eat lots of fruits and vegetables and carbohydrates, like pasta or rice. Keep sweet or fatty foods for treats.

TOP TIP

The next time you need a quick snack, grab an apple or some plain popcorn. They're healthier than chocolate or chips, and just as tasty.

FEELING THIRSTY

Your body needs plenty of water to keep it healthy.

If you don't drink enough, your body can't work properly and you may start feeling ill. Keep a water bottle handy at home or at school. Don't forget to refill it during the day.

Water is great to drink on its own, or you can mix it with your favorite sugar-free drink mix.

Low-fat milk is also good to drink. It's packed with calcium, which helps make your bones and teeth strong.

It's okay to have fruit juice and soda sometimes, but not every day. They're full of sugar and acid, which can rot your teeth. It's best to drink them with a meal. This does less harm to your teeth.

Lots of fruits and vegetables also contain water, along with vital nutrients.

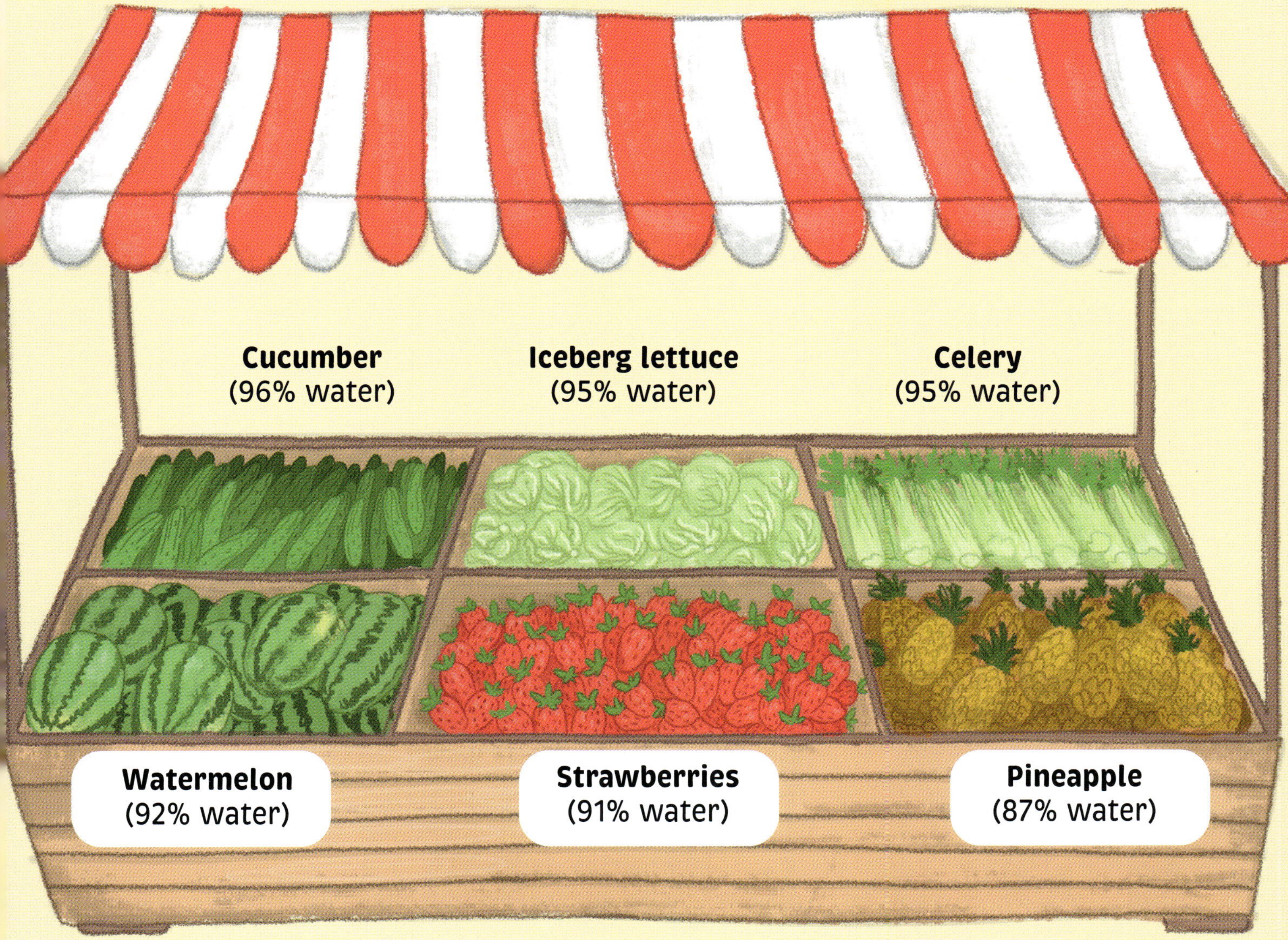

TOP TIP

Try to drink around 5–6 glasses of water a day. You'll need to drink more if the weather's warm or if you're doing sports.

GETTING ACTIVE

Exercise is good for you in lots of different ways.

It makes your body stronger. It keeps your heart and lungs working well. It helps to keep your weight at a healthy level. It also makes you sleep better, and feel happier and calmer.

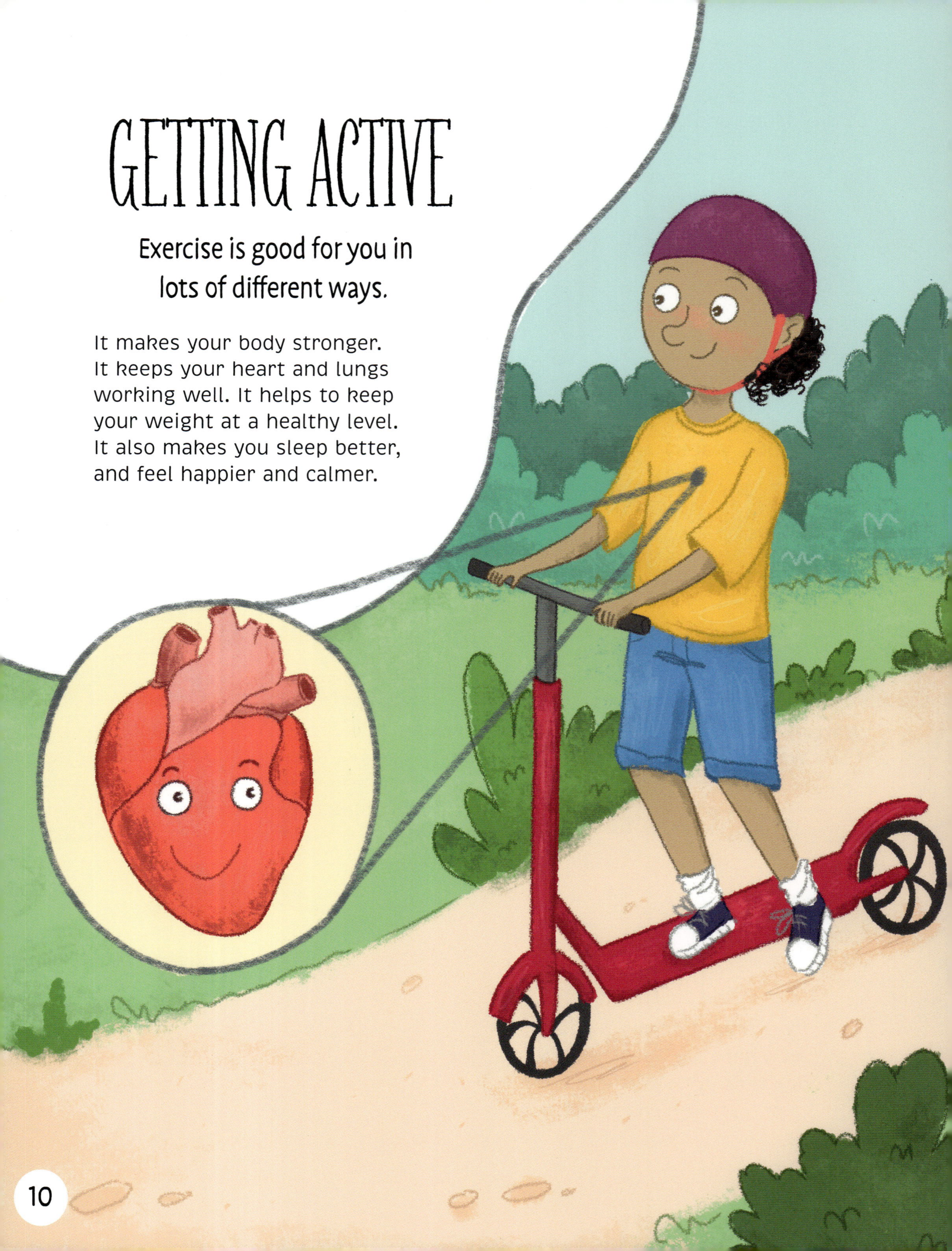

But what if you don't enjoy gym class, or feel too tired to exercise when you come home from school? The trick is to find something you enjoy. That way, you're more likely to stick to it. There are many ideas to try on the next two pages. You can try things like walking or biking to school, taking the dog for a walk, or dancing to your favorite music with a friend.

Try to do some exercise most days, even if you don't feel like it. When you get used to it, you'll find it easier to keep going. You don't have to do it all at once. You can break it up into short chunks to do at different times of the day.

ON THE MOVE

Are you ready to get moving? You don't have to be super sporty. Try out different activities until you find one you really like.

Here are some ideas. With any new exercise, start off gently and build up slowly. This will keep you from getting injured. And don't forget to have fun!

TOP TIP

Teaming up with a fitness buddy will help you stick with exercise. If one of you is feeling tired or fed up, the other can keep you both going.

SLEEP TIGHT

After a busy day, your body needs a break. It needs a good night's sleep. Sleep gives your body a chance to recharge, ready for the next day.

If you don't get enough sleep, you might ...

... feel tired and grumpy

... have trouble thinking clearly

...struggle to stay awake in class.

You might also ...

... find it hard to remember things

... get ill more often

... not grow as much as you should.

Sleep is important for staying healthy, learning, and feeling good. But what happens if you have a hard time nodding off at night? Here are some top sleep tips.

1. Try to go to bed at the same time every night.
2. Have a warm bath, or read a book to relax.
3. Don't do any exercise just before bedtime.
4. Make your bedroom a calm and relaxing space.
5. Turn off any devices at least an hour before going to bed.
6. Close your eyes and count backwards from 100, 99, 98, 97 ...

Some people need more sleep than others. Between the ages of 5 and 12, try to get around 10–11 hours' sleep a night.

DON'T WORRY

You might find it hard to fall asleep if you're worried about something.

Worries can seem worse at night, and go around and around in your mind. It's easy for them to seem bigger and worse than they really are.

Everyone feels worried, scared, or sad sometimes. It's all part of being human. You might have a test coming up at school. You might have had a fight with your best friend. Your family pet might be sick. Looking after your feelings is just as important as looking after your body.

It's important to tell someone if you're feeling down. Don't keep it to yourself. Talk to your mom, dad, or another trusted adult. At school, you can speak to your teacher or the school nurse. Telling someone will make you feel better, and help you find ways of coping with your worries.

STRESS BUSTING

There are lots of things you can do to help yourself feel happier and more positive. Then you can get on with enjoying life!

Do things you enjoy, like seeing your friends.

Z Z Z

Make sure that you get enough sleep.

Get plenty of exercise, especially outdoors.

Eat a healthy diet and drink lots of water.

Drop a sport or hobby if you've got too much going on.

Think about the good stuff, no matter how small.

Remember, it's not just you. Everyone feels down sometimes.

Make a list of things that are worrying you.

Now make a list of things you like about your life.

One way to feel calm is to focus on your breathing. It takes a bit of practice, but it really works.

1. Find a place where you can sit quietly.
2. Breathe in deeply, through your nose.
3. Breathe from your tummy, not your chest.
4. Breathe out slowly, through your mouth.
5. Wait a few seconds, then try it again.

KEEPING CLEAN

Hate the idea of taking a shower? Can't be bothered to hop in the bath? Don't worry – you're not alone!

But keeping your body clean will help you feel better and stay healthier. It's a good idea to wash up every day. This is especially important if you've been running around with friends or playing sports.

If you get into good habits now, it will help as you get older. As you grow up, you start to sweat more and this can cause a smell, called body odor (BO). To prevent this, you'll need to take a shower or bath every day. You'll also need to change your clothes more often, especially your socks and underwear. You should change these every day.

DID YOU KNOW?

Your skin and hair will probably get greasier as you grow up. This is because of oil being made in your skin. You might need to wash your face and hair more often.

HEALTHY TEETH

Are your parents always reminding you to brush your teeth? It's good advice.

Healthy teeth help you to eat, speak, and smile. But sugar and acid in your food can harm your teeth and gums. You might end up with a painful toothache or even have to have a tooth taken out.

To keep your teeth healthy, brush them twice a day. Squeeze a pea-sized blob of toothpaste onto your toothbrush. Brush your teeth for at least two minutes each time (some electric toothbrushes can time this for you). Make sure you brush all of your teeth, not just the front ones. Spit out the toothpaste - don't swallow it.

Don't miss regular checkups at the dentist - you should go twice a year. The dentist will check your teeth and gums. They will also tell you the best way to brush, and help keep your teeth sparkling white and clean.

STAYING WELL

You've been doing a great job of looking after your body. But things can still go wrong sometimes.

Here are some of the most common illnesses you might get, and what they do to your body.

COLD

Caused by: cold viruses

Symptoms: runny nose; sneezing; stuffy nose; watery eyes; cough; feeling tired

If you're feeling ill, make sure you talk to your mom or dad. Many illnesses are easy to treat at home, and will clear up quickly. For more serious problems, your parents might need to take you to see the doctor.

STOMACH BUG

Caused by: a virus or bacteria in food

Symptoms: throwing up; diarrhea; stomachache; fever

TONSILLITIS

Caused by: a virus or bacteria

Symptoms: sore throat; fever; headache; pain when swallowing

WASH YOUR HANDS!

Many illnesses are caused by bacteria or viruses. We also call them germs.

A favorite place for germs to be is on your hands. Whenever you touch things, germs get onto your hands. If you touch your eyes, nose, and mouth afterwards, the germs can get into your body and make you ill.

You can also pass germs on to other people, and they can become ill, too. The best way to stop this happening is to wash your hands often during the day.

Wash your hands with warm water and soap. Make sure you wash the fronts and backs, and in between your fingers. Don't forget your nails. Wash for as long as it takes you to sing "Happy Birthday" twice. Then rinse with warm water, and dry your hands.

WASH YOUR HANDS ...

- before and after meals
- after playing outside
- after touching pets
- after using the bathroom
- after coughing or blowing your nose
- after visiting someone who's ill.

LOOKING AFTER YOU

Your body is very precious.

It does so many things for you and makes you who you are.

It's your job to look after your body and keep it in top condition. That way, it will keep on working hard for you for many years to come.

It's also important to take care of your feelings. Sometimes, things might go wrong. You might find yourself feeling sad, or becoming ill. Don't worry, this is completely normal. Looking after yourself can help to stop some of these things from happening.

If you're worried about anything that's happening to your body, make sure you tell someone you trust. Everybody's body needs a bit of help sometimes. So take good care of it and your amazing body should last you a lifetime!

GLOSSARY

Acid
A chemical in soda that can make your teeth rot.

Bacteria
Tiny living things that can be helpful or harmful.

Body odor (BO)
Smell caused by sweat mixing with bacteria on your skin.

Calcium
A chemical found in some foods, such as cheese or milk, that keeps your teeth and bones strong.

Carbohydrates
Types of starchy foods, such as bread, potatoes, and pasta, that give you energy.

Dairy
Foods that are made from milk, such as butter, cheese, and yogurt.

Energy
Power that makes your body able to do work.

Germs
Bacteria and viruses are both types of germs.

Nutrients
Nourishing parts of foods.

Protein
A nutrient found in foods such as vegetables, fish, nuts, and eggs.

Recharge
Fill with more energy.

Virus
Tiny living thing that can be harmful.

FIND OUT MORE

Websites

kidshealth.org/en/kids/center/htbw-main-page.html

This website features fun, educational videos for kids.

https://www.ducksters.com/science/biology/humanbody.php

Learn more fascinating facts about the human body here.

kidshealth.org/en/kids/grow

This site features answers to many common questions about growing up.

Books

Why Do I Have to: Eat Healthy Food?
by Kay Barnham (Windmill Books, 2024)

Why Do I Have to: Go to Sleep?
by Kay Barnham (Windmill Books, 2024)

Why Do I Have to: Keep Clean?
by Kay Barnham (Windmill Books, 2024)

INDEX